AF489374

LET'S EXPLORE THE FARM

Speedy Publishing LLC
40 E. Main St. #1156
Newark, DE 19711
www.speedypublishing.com

Copyright 2018

All Rights reserved. No part of this book may be reproduced or used in any way or form or by any means whether electronic or mechanical, this means that you cannot record or photocopy any material ideas or tips that are provided in this book.

A farm is an area of land that is devoted primarily to agricultural processes. It is the basic production facility in food production.

Farming is the art of cultivating the soil, growing and harvesting crops, and the raising of animals.

A farm may
be owned and
operated by a
single individual,
family, community
or a company.

A farm may run under a monoculture system or with an array of cereal or arable crops, which may be separate from or mixed with raising livestock.

Dairy farming is a class of agriculture, where female cows, goats, or other mammals are raised for their milk.

Poultry farms are dedicated to raising chickens, turkeys, ducks, and other fowl, generally for meat or eggs.

Farmers of livestock work throughout the year. Animals must be fed and watered daily. Dairy cows must be milked two or three times a day.

Farmers on crop farms usually work from sunrise to sunset during the planting and harvesting seasons. During the rest of the year they plan next season's crops, market their products and repair machinery.

Sheep are farmed
for wool or meat
or milk. Wool is cut
once a year. This
is called shearing,
and people who
do it are called
shearers.

A pig farm is one that specializes in raising pigs or hogs for bacon, ham and other pork products and may be free range, intensive, or both.

Goats are important farm animals all over the world. They can live in mountainous and dry areas where other animals (such as cows) would not be able to live.

www.ingramcontent.com/pod-product-compliance
Lightning Source LLC
Chambersburg PA
CBHW060151120726
48003CB00010B/3108